CARL PHILIPP EMANUEL BACH

Solfeggio

c-Moll / C minor / ut mineur

Wq 117/2 / H220

für Klavier / for Piano / pour piano

Urtext

Herausgegeben von / Edited by / Édition de
Wolfram Enßlin

ALLE RECHTE VORBEHALTEN · ALL RIGHTS RESERVED

EDITION PETERS
LEIPZIG · LONDON · NEW YORK

Inhalt · Contents · Sommaire

Vorwort · Preface · Avant-propos .... III · IV · V

Carl Philipp Emanuel Bach: Solfeggio c-Moll / *Solfeggio C minor* / *Solfeggio ut mineur* 2

Kritische Bemerkungen · Critical Notes · Notes critiques 4

© 2021 by C. F. Peters Ltd & Co. KG, Leipzig
Alle Rechte vorbehalten · All rights reserved
Vervielfältigungen jeglicher Art sind gesetzlich verboten.
Any unauthorized reproduction is prohibited by law.
ISMN 979-0-014-13682-6

Vorwort

Carl Philipp Emanuel Bach komponierte sein *Solfeggio* in c-Moll Wq 117/2[1] (H 220[2]) seinem Clavierwerkeverzeichnis (CV 1772) sowie seinem Nachlassverzeichnis (NV 1790) zufolge 1766 in Potsdam und publizierte es 1770 in dem von ihm selbst herausgegebenen und bei Michael Christian Bock in Hamburg gedruckten Sammelwerk *Musikalisches Vielerley*[3].

C. P. E. Bach hinterließ in seinem umfangreichen kompositorischen Œuvre mehr als 300 Kompositionen für Solo-Clavier[4] und deckte damit alle damals denkbaren Teilgattungen ab, von Sonaten über Rondos, Fantasien und Fugen bis hin zu Charakterstücken und Tänzen sowie zahlreichen weiteren kurzen Einzelsätzen. Darunter befinden sich sechs Stücke, die er als *Solfeggio* bezeichnete.[5] Diese Bezeichnung für eine Clavierkomposition ist insofern bemerkenswert, als darunter gemeinhin ein textloses Übungsstück für Gesang zu verstehen ist. Heinrich Christoph Koch definierte in seinem *Musikalischen Lexikon* ein *Solfeggio* wie folgt:

> „Solfeggio, bezeichnet ein Tonstück zur Uebung im Gesange, welches mit keinem Texte verbunden ist. Man bedient sich solcher Tonstücke, theils um den Anfänger die Intervallen sicher treffen und rein intoniren zu lehren, theils auch um die Gesangorgane des schon geübten Sängers im Vortrage aller Arten die Colloraturen zu üben."[6]

Dass aber nicht nur von Bach Clavierstücke als *Solfeggio* tituliert wurden, zeigt der Eintrag in Daniel Gottlob Türks *Clavierschule oder Anweisung zum Clavierspielen für Lehrer und Lernende*:

> „Das Wort *Solfeggio* wird eigentlich vom Gesange gebraucht, und bezeichnet ein Tonstück zur Uebung im Treffen, nach den bekannten Silben: ut, re, mi, fa, sol, la, (si,) wofür Graun weit schicklicher die folgenden sieben: da, me, ni, po, tu, la, be, wählte. Beym Klavierspielen versteht man unter Solfeggio ebenfalls ein Tonstück, welches blos zur Uebung im Spielen, und um sich Fertigkeit zu erwerben, bestimmt ist. Solfeggiren heißt daher, sich im Treffen oder Spielen schwerer Stellen u. dgl. zu üben."[7]

Der etüdenhafte Charakter ist gerade im *Solfeggio* c-Moll offensichtlich. Andere Solfeggi kommen einer Fantasie nahe (wie etwa Wq 117/3) oder betonen kontrapunktische Eigenheiten (wie das kanonische *Solfeggio* Wq 112/18).

Unter Bachs sechs Solfeggi ist dasjenige in c-Moll das bekannteste und bis heute am häufigsten edierte. Bereits zu Lebzeiten Bachs erfuhr es eine weite Verbreitung. Neben dem Druck sind allein 20 handschriftliche Abschriften (zumeist Druckabschriften) überliefert.[8] Wie häufig bei Bach, wenn ein von ihm autorisierter Druck existiert, fehlt auch hier die autografe Partitur. Diese verlor für ihn durch den Druck an Wichtigkeit, zumeist dürfte er sie selbst entsorgt haben.

Zwischen 1760 und 1770 erschienen in Berlin und Hamburg drei allein schon durch die Ähnlichkeit der Titel aufeinander bezogene Sammlungen als wöchentliche bzw. vierteljährliche Periodika: *Musikalisches Allerley* (Berlin 1760–1763 bei Friedrich Wilhelm Birnstiel), *Musikalisches Mancherley* (Berlin 1762/63 bei George Ludwig Winter) sowie *Musikalisches Vielerley* (Hamburg 1770 durch C. P. E. Bach bei Michael Christian Bock).[9]

Leipzig, im Juli 2020   *Wolfram Enßlin*

---

[1] Alfred Wotquenne, *Thematisches Verzeichnis der Werke von Carl Philipp Emanuel Bach (1714–1788)*, Leipzig 1905, Reprint Wiesbaden 1964.

[2] Eugene Helm, *Thematic Catalogue of the Works of Carl Philipp Emanuel Bach*, New Haven 1989.

[3] CV 1772, Nr. 160: „Pet. Piec. NB [Incipit Fantasie g-Moll, Wq 117/13] P[otsdam]. 66 bestehet aus 3 Fantasien u. 3 Solfeggi" bzw. NV 1790, S. 21: „Clavier-Soli No. 160: P[otsdam]. 1766, bestehet aus 3 Fantasien und 2 [korrekt: 3] Solfeggien, welche im Musikalischen Vielerley gedruckt sind."

[4] „Clavier" gilt hier als allgemeiner Begriff für Tasteninstrument und beinhaltet Instrumente wie Cembalo, Clavichord oder Hammerclavier. Häufig hat Bach, dessen besondere Vorliebe dem Clavichord galt, das für die jeweilige Clavierkomposition intendierte Instrument nicht explizit erwähnt. Fast 350 Clavierkompositionen, mitsamt einiger bezüglich seiner Autorschaft unsicheren Kompositionen, vor allem aus Bachs Jugendzeit, beinhaltet das kurz vor der Fertigstellung befindliche neue Instrumentalwerkeverzeichnis C. P. E. Bachs (*Carl Philipp Emanuel Bach: Thematisch-systematisches Verzeichnis der musikalischen Werke Teil 1: Instrumentalwerke*, bearbeitet von Wolfram Enßlin [= Bach-Repertorium. Werkverzeichnisse zur Musikerfamilie Bach, hrsg. vom Bach-Archiv Leipzig, Bd. III.1]).

[5] *Solfeggio* G-Dur, Wq 112/4, *Solfeggio* C-Dur, Wq 112/10, und *Solfeggio* G-Dur, Wq 112/18, wurden jeweils 1759 in Berlin komponiert und erschienen 1765 in der Sammlung *Clavierstücke verschiedener Art* in Berlin bei G. L. Winter im Druck. Zusammen mit dem *Solfeggio* c-Moll entstanden die *Solfeggi* Es-Dur und A-Dur, Wq 117/3–4, im Jahr 1766 in Potsdam und wurden im *Musikalischen Vielerley* publiziert. Die in zahlreichen Ausgaben anzutreffende Bezeichnung *Solfeggietto* für Wq 117/2 geht nicht auf Carl Philipp Emanuel Bach zurück. Sie tauchte wohl Ende des 19./Anfang des 20. Jahrhunderts das erste Mal auf, beispielsweise in einer Ausgabe von Oscar Wagner bei Augener (London).

[6] Heinrich Christoph Koch, *Musicalisches Lexikon*, Frankfurt (Main) 1802, Sp. 1399, Reprint Kassel 2001.

[7] Daniel Gottlob Türk, *Clavierschule oder Anweisung zum Clavierspielen für Lehrer und Lernende*, Leipzig/Halle 1789, S. 398, Reprint Kassel 1997.

[8] Die Abschriften befinden sich heute in Bibliotheken in Berlin, Bonn, Brüssel, Cambridge (GB), Hamburg, New Haven (USA), Prag, Schwerin und Wien.

[9] Siehe hierzu Ulrich Leisinger, „Musikalisches Allerley, Mancherley, Vielerley – Drei gedruckte Sammlungen mit Hausmusik aus der zweiten Hälfte des 18. Jahrhunderts", in: *Hausmusik im 17. und 18. Jahrhundert*, hrsg. von Christian Philipsen in Verbindung mit Ute Omonsky, Augsburg 2016, S. 233–244.

Preface

According to Carl Philipp Emanuel Bach's catalogue of keyboard works (Clavierwerkeverzeichnis, CV 1772) and the catalogue of his effects (Nachlassverzeichnis, NV 1790), he composed his *Solfeggio* in C minor Wq 117/2[1] (H220[2]) in 1766 in Potsdam. It was published by Michael Christian Bock in Hamburg in 1770 in the collection *Musikalisches Vielerley*[3] which Bach himself edited.

In his extensive output, C. P. E. Bach wrote more than 300 compositions for solo keyboard (clavier)[4] covering every possible genre and sub-genre – from sonatas to rondos, fantasias and fugues, to character pieces and dances, as well as numerous other short individual movements. These include six pieces which he called *Solfeggio*.[5] This description for a keyboard composition is unusual, as it is generally used to refer to a study for voice without text. Heinrich Christoph Koch defined *solfeggio* as follows in his *Musikalisches Lexikon*:

> 'Solfeggio describes a piece of music for practising singing which has no text. One uses such pieces of music partly in order to help beginners sing intervals with accuracy and to teach pure intonation, and partly also for established singers to practise their vocal skills in performing all kinds of coloratura.'[6]

But it was not only keyboard pieces by Bach that carried the title *Solfeggio*, as shown by the entry in Daniel Gottlob Türk's *Clavierschule oder Anweisung zum Clavierspielen für Lehrer und Lernende*:

> 'The word *solfeggio* is actually used in singing, and describes a piece of music for practising intervals using the familiar syllables: ut, re, mi, fa, sol, la, (si,) instead of which, Graun chose the following and far more appropriate seven: da, me, ni, po, tu, la, be. In keyboard playing, *solfeggio* is likewise understood to mean a piece of music which is solely intended for practising playing, and for acquiring skill. Solfeggiren [to vocalize] therefore means to practise singing or playing difficult passages & the like.'[7]

The etude-like character is especially evident in the *Solfeggio* in C minor. Other *solfeggi* are more fantasia-like (such as Wq 117/3) or emphasize contrapuntal characteristics (such as the canonic *Solfeggio* Wq 112/18).

Of Bach's six *solfeggi* the one in C minor is the best known and the most frequently published to date. Even during Bach's lifetime it enjoyed wide circulation. As well as the printed edition, 20 manuscript copies survive (mainly hand-written copies of printed editions).[8] As is frequently the case with Bach, when a printed edition authorized by him exists, the autograph score is missing. These had become less important for him because of the printed editions, and he may usually have discarded them himself.

Between 1760 and 1770, three periodicals were published weekly or quarterly in Berlin and Hamburg, the similarity of their titles alone showing their relation to each other: *Musikalisches Allerley* (published in Berlin in 1760–1763 by Friedrich Wilhelm Birnstiel), *Musikalisches Mancherley* (published in Berlin in 1762/63 by George Ludwig Winter) and *Musikalisches Vielerley* (edited by C. P. E. Bach and published in Hamburg in 1770 by Michael Christian Bock).[9]

Leipzig, July 2020

Wolfram Enßlin
(Translation: Elizabeth Robinson)

---

[1] Alfred Wotquenne, *Thematisches Verzeichnis der Werke von Carl Philipp Emanuel Bach (1714–1788)*, Leipzig 1905, reprint Wiesbaden 1964.

[2] Eugene Helm, *Thematic Catalogue of the Works of Carl Philipp Emanuel Bach*, New Haven 1989.

[3] CV 1772, No. 160: 'Pet. Piec. NB [incipit of the Fantasia in G minor, Wq 117/13] P[otsdam]. 66 bestehet aus 3 Fantasien u. 3 Solfeggi' (comprises 3 Fantasias & 3 Solfeggi) and NV 1790, p. 21: 'Clavier-Soli No. 160: P[otsdam]. 1766, bestehet aus 3 Fantasien und 2 [in fact: 3] Solfeggien, welche im Musikalischen Vielerley gedruckt sind' (comprises 3 Fantasias and 2 [in fact: 3] solfeggi, which are published in the Musikalisches Vielerley).

[4] Here, the word 'keyboard' ('Clavier') is the general term for keyboard instruments, and includes instruments such as harpsichord, clavichord and fortepiano. Bach, who was particularly fond of the clavichord, often did not specify the instrument he had in mind for a particular keyboard composition. The new catalogue of C. P. E. Bach's instrumental works (*Carl Philipp Emanuel Bach: Thematisch-systematisches Verzeichnis der musikalischen Werke Teil 1: Instrumentalwerke*, edited by Wolfram Enßlin [= Bach-Repertorium. Werkverzeichnisse zur Musikerfamilie Bach, ed. Bach-Archiv Leipzig, Vol. III.1], in preparation) contains nearly 350 keyboard compositions, including some of uncertain authorship, particularly from Bach's youth.

[5] *Solfeggio* in G major, Wq 112/4, *Solfeggio* in C major, Wq 112/10, and *Solfeggio* in G major, Wq 112/18, were all composed in 1759 in Berlin and published by G. L. Winter in 1765 in the collection *Clavierstücke verschiedener Art* in Berlin. Together with the *Solfeggio* in C minor, the *Solfeggi* in E flat major and A major, Wq 117/3–4, were composed in 1766 in Potsdam and published in *Musikalisches Vielerley*. The description *Solfeggietto* for Wq 117/2 found in numerous editions was not given by Carl Philipp Emanuel Bach. It probably emerged for the first time at the end of the 19th / beginning of the 20th century, for example in an edition by Oscar Wagner published by Augener (London).

[6] Heinrich Christoph Koch, *Musicalisches Lexikon*, Frankfurt (Main) 1802, col. 1399, reprint Kassel 2001.

[7] Daniel Gottlob Türk, *Clavierschule oder Anweisung zum Clavierspielen für Lehrer und Lernende*, Leipzig / Halle 1789, p. 398, reprint Kassel 1997.

[8] The copies are now preserved in libraries in Berlin, Bonn, Brussels, Cambridge (GB), Hamburg, New Haven (USA), Prague, Schwerin and Vienna.

[9] For information on this, see Ulrich Leisinger, '*Musikalisches Allerley, Mancherley, Vielerley* – Drei gedruckte Sammlungen mit Hausmusik aus der zweiten Hälfte des 18. Jahrhunderts', in: *Hausmusik im 17. und 18. Jahrhundert*, ed. Christian Philipsen in collaboration with Ute Omonsky, Augsburg 2016, pp. 233–244.

Avant-propos

D'après son catalogue d'œuvres pour clavier (*Clavierwerkeverzeichnis*, CV 1772) et l'inventaire de sa succession (*Nachlassverzeichnis*, NV 1790), Carl Philipp Emanuel Bach a composé son Solfeggio en *ut* mineur Wq 117/2[1] (H 220[2]) en 1766 à Potsdam et l'a édité lui-même en 1770 dans un recueil intitulé *Musikalisches Vielerley*[3] imprimé par Michael Christian Bock à Hambourg.

C. P. E. Bach a laissé dans son vaste catalogue de compositions plus de 300 pièces pour clavier seul[4], couvrant tous les genres imaginables à l'époque, de la sonate à la pièce de caractère et à la danse, en passant par le rondo, la fantaisie et la fugue, outre de nombreuses autres pièces brèves isolées. Parmi elles s'en trouvent six qu'il baptise *solfeggio*[5]. Pour une pièce de clavier cette appellation est inhabituelle, dans la mesure où elle désigne généralement un exercice vocal sans texte. Heinrich Christoph Koch définit ainsi le *solfeggio* dans son *Musikalisches Lexikon* :

> « *Solfeggio* désigne une pièce de musique destinée à l'exercice vocal sans aucun texte associé. On utilise ce genre de pièce aussi bien pour apprendre aux débutants à lire sûrement les intervalles et à les entonner avec justesse que pour exercer l'organe vocal du chanteur déjà formé à exécuter toute sorte de coloratures[6]. »

Mais Bach ne fut pas le seul à intituler des pièces pour clavier *solfeggio*, comme le montre cette remarque dans la *Clavierschule oder Anweisung zum Clavierspielen für Lehrer und Lernende* de Daniel Gottlob Türk :

> « Le mot *solfeggio* est utilisé proprement pour le chant et désigne une pièce destinée à servir d'exercice de lecture sur les syllabes connues *ut, ré, mi, fa, sol, la, (si)*, que Graun choisit bien plus judicieusement de remplacer par les suivantes : *da, me, ni, po, tu, la, be*. Au clavier, on entend par *solfeggio* une pièce musicale destinée uniquement à s'exercer au jeu et à acquérir de la dextérité. Solfier [*solfeggiren*] signifie donc s'exercer à lire ou à jouer des passages difficiles et des choses de ce genre[7].

Le caractère d'étude est particulièrement évident dans le *Solfeggio* en *ut* mineur. D'autres *solfeggi* se rapprochent de la fantaisie (comme par exemple Wq 117/3) ou mettent l'accent sur l'écriture contrapuntique (comme le *Solfeggio* canonique Wq 112/18).

Parmi les six *solfeggi* de Bach, celui en *ut* mineur est le plus connu et le plus souvent publié jusqu'à présent. Déjà du vivant de Bach il connut une large diffusion. En plus de l'édition imprimée, vingt copies manuscrites nous sont parvenues (la plupart faites d'après l'édition imprimée)[8]. Comme souvent chez Bach, lorsqu'il existe une édition autorisée par lui, la partition autographe manque. Celle-ci perdait de son importance pour lui du fait de l'édition imprimée, et il est possible qu'il s'en soit parfois séparé lui-même.

Entre 1760 et 1770 paraissaient à Berlin et à Hambourg trois périodiques hebdomadaires ou trimestriels dont les titres similaires révèlent les parentés : *Musikalisches Allerley* (Berlin 1760–1763, chez Friedrich Wilhelm Birnstiel), *Musikalisches Mancherley* (Berlin 1762–1763, chez George Ludwig Winter) et *Musikalisches Vielerley* (Hambourg 1770, édition de C. P. E. Bach chez Michael Christian Bock)[9].

Leipzig, juillet 2020

Wolfram Enßlin
(traduction : Dennis Collins)

---

[1] Alfred Wotquenne, *Thematisches Verzeichnis der Werke von Carl Philipp Emanuel Bach (1714–1788)*, Leipzig 1905, reprint Wiesbaden 1964.

[2] Eugene Helm, *Thematic Catalogue of the Works of Carl Philipp Emanuel Bach*, New Haven 1989.

[3] CV 1772, No. 160 : « Pet. Piec. NB [Incipit Fantaisie *sol* mineur, Wq 117/13] P[otsdam]. 66 bestehet aus 3 Fantasien u. 3 Solfeggi » (se compose de 3 Fantaisies et 3 Solfeggi) resp. NV 1790, p. 21 : « Clavier-Soli No. 160 : P[otsdam]. 1766, bestehet aus 3 Fantasien und 2 [*recte* : 3] Solfeggien, welche im Musikalischen Vielerley gedruckt sind » (se compose de 3 Fantaisie et 2 [*recte* : 3] Solfeggi, imprimées dans la collection *Musikalisches Vielerley*).

[4] « Clavier » est ici un terme générique pour tout instrument à clavier, que ce soit le clavecin, le clavicorde ou le piano-forte. Bach, qui avait une prédilection particulière pour le clavicorde, n'indique en général pas explicitement l'instrument auquel il destine ses pièces pour clavier. Le nouveau catalogue des œuvres instrumentales de C. P. E. Bach, en préparation (*Carl Philipp Emanuel Bach : Thematisch-systematisches Verzeichnis der musikalischen Werke Teil 1 : Instrumentalwerke*, éd. Wolfram Enßlin [= Bach-Repertorium. Werkverzeichnisse zur Musikerfamilie Bach, Bach-Archiv Leipzig, vol. III.1]), comporte près de 350 compositions pour clavier, dont quelques pièces d'attribution incertaine datant avant tout de la jeunesse du compositeur.

[5] Le *Solfeggio* en *sol* majeur, Wq 112/4, le *Solfeggio* en *ut* majeur, Wq 112/10, et le *Solfeggio* en *sol* majeur, Wq 112/18, ont été composés en 1759 à Berlin et publiés en 1765 dans le recueil de *Clavierstücke verschiedener Art*, à Berlin, chez G. L. Winter. Le *Solfeggio* en *ut* mineur, ainsi que les *Solfeggi* en *mi* bémol majeur et en *la* majeur, Wq 117/3–4, ont vu le jour à Potsdam en 1766 et ont été publiés dans le *Musikalisches Vielerley*. Le titre *Solfeggietto* qu'on voit dans beaucoup d'éditions pour Wq 117/2 n'émane pas de Carl Philipp Emanuel Bach. Il est apparu pour les premières fois à la fin du XIXᵉ siècle et au début du XXᵉ siècle, par exemple dans une édition d'Oscar Wagner chez Augener (Londres).

[6] Heinrich Christoph Koch, *Musicalisches Lexikon*, Francfort-sur-le-Main 1802, col. 1399, reprint Cassel 2001.

[7] Daniel Gottlob Türk, *Clavierschule oder Anweisung zum Clavierspielen für Lehrer und Lernende*, Leipzig / Halle 1789, p. 398, reprint Cassel 1997.

[8] Les copies se trouvent maintenant dans des bibliothèques à Berlin, Bonn, Bruxelles, Cambridge (GB), Hambourg, New Haven (États-Unis), Prague, Schwerin et Vienne.

[9] À ce sujet, voir Ulrich Leisinger, « *Musikalisches Allerley, Mancherley, Vielerley* – Drei gedruckte Sammlungen mit Hausmusik aus der zweiten Hälfte des 18. Jahrhunderts », in *Hausmusik im 17. und 18. Jahrhundert*, éd. Christian Philipsen en collaboration avec Ute Omonsky, Augsbourg 2016, p. 233–244.

Solfeggio

c-Moll / C minor / ut mineur

Carl Philipp Emanuel Bach (1714–1788)
Wq 117/2 / H220

*) Siehe Kritische Bemerkungen (S. 4) / *See Critical Notes (p. 4)* / *Voir Notes critiques (p. 4)*

Edition Peters 11635   34859   © 2021 by C. F. Peters Ltd & Co. KG, Leipzig

**) Ausführung des prallenden Doppelschlags:
    Execution of the turn with upper mordent:
    Exécution du demi-tremblement doublé :

Kritische Bemerkungen

Der von C. P. E. Bach durch seine Herausgeberschaft autorisierte Druck im *Musikalischen Vielerley* dient als einzige Quelle für diese Edition.

Die Titelseite der aus 104 Blättern bestehenden Sammlung lautet[1]: „*Musikalisches Vielerley.* | *Herausgegeben* | *von* | *Herrn Carl Philip Emanuel Bach,* | *Musik=Director zu Hamburg.* | *Hamburg,*| *gedruckt und verlegt von Michael Christian Bock.* | 1770." (Titelseite, S. 2 leer, S. 3 u. 4 Inhalt. p. 1 (*Erstes Stück*) – p. 204 (*Ein und funfzigstes Stück*).

Das Solfeggio befindet sich auf p. 19 und besitzt den Kopftitel: *Musikalisches Vielerley. Fünftes Stück.* | SOLFEGGIO. *Vom Herrn Capellmeister Bach, in Hamburg.* Das obere System ist im Sopranschlüssel notiert.

Die Edition folgt weitgehend der originalen Balkensetzung, verzichtet aber bei gemeinsam balkierten Gruppen auf den Wechsel zwischen den Systemen. Die Artikulationsligatur am Ende von Takt 25 im oberen System entspricht einem prallenden Doppelschlag. Der Ausführungsvorschlag folgt C. P. E. Bachs eigener Beschreibung in seinem *Versuch über die wahre Art das Clavier zu spielen* (Teil 1, Berlin 1753), p. 93 (Das zweyte Hauptstück, vierte Abtheilung *Von dem Doppelschlage* § 28 mit dazugehörigen Tabula V, Fig. LXIII).

Die damals übliche Regel bei der Akzidenziensetzung, dass das Akzidenz – anders als heute – nicht für den gesamten Takt gilt, sondern vor jeder betreffenden Note wiederholt wurde, ist von C. P. E. Bach im Druck nicht konsequent umgesetzt worden. Die Takte 7 und 8 spiegeln insgesamt diese inkonsequente Akzidenziensetzung wider. Dadurch bleibt zumindest bei der zwölften und sechzehnten Note in Takt 7 ein gewisses Fragezeichen. Es hätte eines Auflösungszeichens bedurft, um das ansonsten über den Takten 7 und 8 „orgelpunktartig" vorhandene (und musikalisch wahrscheinlichere) a^1 anzuzeigen und nicht für die zwölfte und sechzehnte Note ein as^1 spielen zu lassen, was allerdings bei dem immer wieder für harmonische Überraschungen sorgenden Komponisten Bach nicht gänzlich auszuschließen wäre.

[1] Die Sammlung ist in folgenden Bibliotheken nachgewiesen (nach RISM-Siglen): B-Bc, D-B, D-EIb, D-G, D-HAu, D-KIl, D-LEm, F-Pn, GB-LBl, NL-DHgm, US-AAu, US-Bp, US-NH, US-R, US-Wc. Vom Brüsseler Exemplar aus dem ehemaligen Besitz des C. P. E. Bach-Sammlers Johann Jacob Heinrich Westphal existiert eine Faksimile-Ausgabe mit einer Einführung von Greta Haenen, Alamire 1993 (= Brussels Royal Conservatory of Music 9).

Critical Notes

The printed edition in *Musikalisches Vielerley*, which has the status of being authorized by C. P. E. Bach as he edited the periodical, serves as the sole source for this edition.

The title page of the collection, which comprises 104 folios, is[1]: '*Musikalisches Vielerley.* | *Herausgegeben* | *von* | *Herrn Carl Philip Emanuel Bach,* | *Musik=Director zu Hamburg.* | *Hamburg,*| *gedruckt und verlegt von Michael Christian Bock.* | 1770.' (Title page, p. 2 blank, pp. 3 & 4 contents. p. 1 (*Erstes Stück*) – p. 204 (*Ein und funfzigstes Stück*).

The *Solfeggio* is found on page 19 and has the title heading: *Musikalisches Vielerley. Fünftes Stück.* | SOLFEGGIO. *Vom Herrn Capellmeister Bach, in Hamburg.* The upper stave is notated in the soprano clef.

The present edition largely follows the original beaming, but when groups of notes are beamed together, avoids changing between the staves. The combined ornamentation at the end of bar 25 in the upper stave may be interpreted as a turn with upper mordent. This performance suggestion follows C. P. E. Bach's own description in his *Versuch über die wahre Art das Clavier zu spielen* (Part 1, Berlin 1753), p. 93 (Das zweyte Hauptstück, vierte Abtheilung *Von dem Doppelschlage* § 28 mit dazugehörigen Tabula V, Fig. LXIII).

The customary rule at the time regarding the placement of accidentals, that the accidental did not apply to the whole bar but was repeated before each note to which it applied (unlike today), was not applied consistently in the printed edition by C. P. E. Bach. Bars 7 and 8 as a whole reflect this inconsistent placement of accidentals. This leaves a question regarding at least the twelfth and the following sixteenth note in bar 7. A natural sign would have been required for the a^1, which is otherwise present through bars 7 and 8 like a pedal point, in order for the twelfth and following sixteenth note not to be played as ab^1; while the natural is more likely, ab^1 cannot be entirely ruled out with a composer such as Bach, who frequently provided harmonic surprises.

[1] The collection is found in the following libraries (RISM sigla): B-Bc, D-B, D-EIb, D-G, D-HAu, D-KIl, D-LEm, F-Pn, GB-LBl, NL-DHgm, US-AAu, US-Bp, US-NH, US-R, US-Wc. A facsimile edition exists of the Brussels copy formerly owned by the C. P. E. Bach collector Johann Jacob Heinrich Westphal with an introduction by Greta Haenen, Alamire 1993 (= Brussels Royal Conservatory of Music 9).

Notes critiques

L'impression de *Musikalisches Vielerley,* approuvée par C. P. E. Bach dans la mesure où il en était l'éditeur, est l'unique source pour la présente édition.

La page de titre de ce recueil composé de 104 folios est : « *Musikalisches Vielerley.* | *Herausgegeben* | *von* | *Herrn Carl Philip Emanuel Bach,* | *Musik=Director zu Hamburg.* | *Hamburg,* | *gedruckt und verlegt von Michael Christian Bock.* | 1770[1]. » (Page de titre, p. 2 blanche, p. 3 et 4 sommaire, p. 1 (1re pièce) – p. 204 (51e pièce).

Le *Solfeggio* se trouve p. 19 sous l'en-tête suivant : *Musikalisches Vielerley. Fünftes Stück.* | SOLFEGGIO. *Vom Herrn Capellmeister Bach, in Hamburg.* La portée supérieure est notée en clef d'ut première.

La présente édition suit dans une large mesure la disposition originale des ligatures, mais évite les groupes ligaturés à cheval sur les deux portées. La liaison à la fin de la mesure 25 à la portée supérieure correspond à un *prallender Doppelschlag* (« demi-tremblement doublé »). L'exécution proposée suit la description donnée par C. P. E. Bach dans son *Versuch über die wahre Art das Clavier zu spielen* (première partie, Berlin 1753), p. 93 (Das zweyte Hauptstück, vierte Abtheilung *Von dem Doppelschlage* § 28 mit dazugehörigen Tabula V, Fig. LXIII).

La règle alors en usage pour le placement des altérations, selon laquelle l'altération, contrairement aux conventions actuelles, ne vaut pas pour l'ensemble de la mesure et doit donc être répétée pour chaque note affectée, n'est pas appliquée de manière conséquente par C. P. E. Bach dans son édition. Les mesures 7 et 8 reflètent ce placement inconséquent des altérations. Il reste de ce fait au moins une interrogation pour la douzième et la seizième note à la mesure 7. Il aurait fallu un bécarre pour faire de ces deux notes un la^3 (musicalement plus vraisemblable), formant une espèce de « pédale » aux mesures 7 et 8, et non un $la b^3$, lequel ne peut cependant être entièrement exclu chez un compositeur comme Bach qui affectionnait les surprises harmoniques.

[1] Le recueil est conservé dans les bibliothèques suivantes (sigles du RISM) : B-Bc, D-B, D-EIb, D-G, D-HAu, D-KIl, D-LEm, F-Pn, GB-LBl, NL-DHgm, US-AAu, US-Bp, US-NH, US-R, US-Wc. Il existe une édition en fac-similé de l'exemplaire de Bruxelles ayant appartenu au collectionneur Johann Jacob Heinrich Westphal, avec une introduction de Greta Haenen, Alamire 1993 (= Brussels Royal Conservatory of Music 9).